P9-EKJ-708

THE FONDUE COOKBOOK
All Rights Reserved

© Pacific Productions
San Francisco, Calif.

1968

Published by

NITTY GRITTY PRODUCTIONS
Concord; Calif.

Distributed by

MAXCY & ASSOCIATES
Los Angeles

The

FONDUE

COOKBOOK

The author wishes to thank the following persons
whose efforts made this book possible.

Hester Callahan
Phoebe MacAdams
Maxcy Callahan

Illustrations by

Howard Sanders

CONTENTS

Fondue is not only a delicious meal, it is a social event. And it is the social element of this versatile dish that makes it truly unique. Today, all over the world, pleasant evenings are being spent among friends preparing and enjoying La Fondue. Its name is French — from the word fondre *which means* to melt *— but the Swiss can claim the credit for having originated fondue. Any account of its history must only be surmised since this dish of melted cheese seems to have evolved through a long period of time; there is no record of any individual being its originator.*

The peasant custom of all eating out of the same pot is, of course, not unique to Switzerland or even Europe. It is practiced in many countries, by many a family too poor to afford individual plates and utensils. But in Switzerland this custom was combined

1

with the circumstances of geography, climate, and a goodly amount of inventiveness, to create a dish which has now become a world-wide favorite. That the national dish of Switzerland should be mainly made of cheese is no surprise; dairy products are of primary importance to this tiny country. The other major element of fondue — bread — is also a natural, bread, too, being an important part of the Swiss diet. Both bread and cheese were made in the summer and fall to be eaten during the winter months. Primitive methods of storage caused them to become hard but not inedible. By melting the cheese, they made it soft and manageable; by dipping the bread in the hot, bubbly cheese, they made it soft enough to chew. Modern recipes still call for stale bread or at least suggest that it be toasted. Although technically fondue means melted, the word has taken on a broader connotation and now popularly implies not just the dish itself but the entire ritual that surrounds it. Thus Beef Bourguignonne and other dishes that do not actually involve melting are, in popular usage, referred to as fondues. In the traditional sense this usage is incorrect. But since the dishes are in great demand, and since they are generally, if mistakenly, referred to as fondue, they will be included in The Fondue Cookbook. The author simply wishes to point out that these are not true fondues.

There is a great deal of ritual involved in the preparation and the eating of fondue. Of course it is possible to break every rule and still delight in the gastronomic pleasures of this savory dish. But in order to enjoy fondue in the traditional way, the ritual should be followed as closely as possible.

Fondue is prepared in the presence of guests. The guests might even be asked to participate in the preparation by chopping cheese or mixing herbs and spices. Conversation is the main ingredient in this step. A little white wine served at this time will help to heighten the taste of the fondue; it should be served at room temperature, not chilled. When the cheese is bubbling lightly the first guest begins by spearing a chunk of bread with a specially designed fondue fork. He gently swirls the bread in the melted cheese in a figure-eight pattern, not in a circle. When the bread is suitably coated, he eats it. Then the process is repeated around the table, each person taking his turn in order.

There are various traditions surrounding the unfortunate person who drops his bread in the fondue pot. The mildest form of punish-

ment is simply the loss of a turn. Perhaps the most enjoyable punishment is for the ladies; if they drop their bread they must kiss each of the men at the table. If a man drops his bread in the fondue, he must buy the wine. Perhaps this is a good place to point out that although it is popularly thought that the participant in the Fondue consumes copious quantities of wine, tradition states that a small glass is drunk during preparation and another during a pause, midway through the entire process.

Ingredients

The following is the recipe for the classic or traditional fondue.

½ pound Emmentaler	1 Tablespoon lemon juice
½ pound Gruyere	3 Tablespoons Kirsh
3 Tablespoons flour	Nutmeg and paprika to taste

1 clove garlic   1 loaf French bread
2 cups dry white wine

Cheese is the most important ingredient in fondue. Those most commonly used are Emmentaler, usually referred to simply as Swiss cheese, and Gruyere. These cheese are both aged; older cheeses resist better the tendency to become stringy. They are also popular because they are highly aromatic when heated. The most important thing to remember, no matter what cheese is called for, is to dice the cheese, not grate it. Diced cheese melts better and more smoothly. However, if a recipe calls for grated cheese it should be grated very coarsely. Also, be sure that heat remains low or the cheese will become stringy, no matter how much care was taken in the choosing and dicing.

The traditional fondue calls for a clove of garlic. It should be cut in half and rubbed along the inside of the cooking pot and on the cooking utensils.

The wine used must be harmonious with the cheese. In some recipes a specific type of wine is named. If the recipe is not specific, any dry white wine is perfectly acceptable. Whatever wine is used in the actual cooking of the fondue should also be drunk in accompaniment. Some recipes also call for Kirsh. Brandy may be substituted if you so desire.

Modern recipes usually call for Italian or French bread. In cutting the bread try to leave each chunk with a crusty side. Originally the bread used was just whatever type happened to be available. Also, chunks of boiled potatoes were once as popular as bread.

7

Potatoes could still provide an interesting alternative.

Implements

In Switzerland, fondue is made in a large round pot called a caquelon. Smaller aluminum fondue pots are now readily available and rather inexpensive. Of course it is not necessary to prepare a fondue in any kind of "official" dish. Almost anything can be used as long as it is round and holds heat well and distributes it evenly; and of course it should remain over an alcohol flame, a candle, or even a hot plate.

A wooden spoon should always be used in stirring the fondue. And it should be stirred always in a figure-eight motion, not in a circle. Circular stirring tends to prevent the full blending of ingredients due to the thickness of the cheese mixture.

The special fondue forks are also optional, although many inexpensive sets are available on the market today. A regular kitchen fork or even a sharp stick would serve the same purpose. However, it should be remembered that the more decorative the dish and other elements, the more festive the effect.

In my view fondue is an innovative dish. You may discard or modify any and all rules to suit your tastes. As long as the basic attractions of socializing and a communal pot remain you are participating in "The Fondue".

An evening with friends spent in enjoyment of a delicious social meal is a most enjoyable goal.

Ed Callahan

FONDUE ROYALE (a Champagne fondue)

2 canned Truffles, sliced

2 cups Champagne

1 lb. grated Swiss Cheese, dredged in Flour

2 Egg yolks

White Pepper to taste

Keep Truffle liquor in can. Warm Truffles in 1⅔ cups Champagne. Add Cheese. Stir until smooth. Add Egg yolks beaten with Truffle liquor and remaining Champagne. Stir into Cheese and blend well. Stir in seasonings. Serves six.

LOBSTER FONDUE

1 lb. Lobster Meat, cut in 1" cubes
2 chopped Truffles
3 Egg Yolks
    Salt, Cayenne, Paprika to taste

2 tbs. Butter
1 cup Cream
Sherry to taste

Melt the Butter and sauté the Truffles for a short time. Add the cubed Lobster, the Sherry and the Seasonings. Beat the Egg Yolks and add the Cream to them. Blend this mixture into the other ingredients. Stir until smooth.

12

FONDUE A LA GEORGIANA

4 oz. grated Gruyère or
   Cheshire Cheese, fresh
6 Eggs
1 Garlic Clove

2 oz. Butter
Salt, Paprika, Cayenne, Parsley
   to taste

Rub the bottom and sides of a chafing dish with a peeled Garlic Clove. Beat the Eggs well and heat on a low flame. Add the Butter and Cheese. Stir constantly until the Cheese has melted and the mixture is thick and smooth. Add the Seasonings and blend in well. Sprinkle a chopped Parsley sprig on the top for color.

WITH HORSERADISH

½ lb. diced cheddar cheese

1 tbs. butter

⅓ cup milk

1 tsp. Worcestershire

¾ tsp. horseradish

½ tsp. salt

pepper to taste

1 egg, separated

2 tbs. sherry

paprika

Melt cheese and butter. Add milk and seasonings. Stir well over low heat until thickened. Add beaten yolk. Cook for a few minutes. Remove from heat. Fold in egg white, beaten stiff. Add sherry and blend.

TOMATO FONDUE

1 sliced Onion	2 chopped medium Tomatoes
3 tbs. Butter	3 tbs. chopped Parsley
1 crushed Garlic Clove	3 tbs. grated Parmesan Cheese
¼ tsp. Thyme Leaves	Salt, Pepper to taste

Melt the Butter and sauté the sliced Onion for 5 minutes. Add the Garlic Clove, Thyme, Tomatoes and the Seasonings. Stir and cook for 30 minutes over a low flame. Add the Parsley and the Cheese and stir until the mixture is thick and smooth.

WITH CAERPHILLY

2 cups Caerphilly Cheese   2 tbs. Flour, ½ tsp. Salt
1½ cups Milk   2 tbs. Butter
    Pepper to taste   1 Garlic Clove

Rub the bottom and sides of the top of a double-boiler chafing dish with a peeled Garlic Clove. Melt the Butter. Add flour and butter to warmed milk. Stir over hot water until smooth. Add the Cheese and stir constantly until the Cheese has melted and the mixture is thick and creamy. Add the Seasonings and blend in well.

FONDUE SONOMA

1 clove Garlic
2 cups California Riesling
1 lb. shredded Swiss Cheese
   Flour

½ tsp. Salt
   pinch Pepper
3 tbs. California Brandy

Rub fondue pot and wooden spoon with Garlic. Heat the Wine but be careful not to boil. Dredge Cheese with Flour. Slowly add Cheese to Wine, stir until bubbly. Add seasonings. Stir in Brandy. Serves 6.

FONDUE AVEC OEUFS

6 hard-boiled Eggs

3 tbs. chopped Parsley

¾ cup Bread Crumbs

2 tbs. chopped Chives

Dill Weed, Salt, Cayenne or Black Pepper, and Paprika to taste.

Halve the hard-boiled Eggs. Remove the Yolks and mash them with the Bread Crumbs and the Seasonings. Stuff the Eggs and pour your favorite fondue over them.

FONDUE DE BERNE

1 lb. 3 ozs. grated Emmenthal Cheese   1 Garlic Clove
½ cup dry White Wine   2½ ozs. Cream
Nutmeg, Paprika to taste   4 Egg Yolks

Rub the bottom and sides of a chafing dish with a peeled Garlic Clove. Heat the Wine until bubbly but not boiling. Add the Cheese and stir constantly until the mixture is smooth. Add the Egg Yolks which have been beaten and combined with the Cream. Blend. Add the Seasonings and stir until the mixture is thick and creamy.

FONDUE MARSEILLAISE (a shrimp fondue)

1 lb. cooked Shrimp

2 cups Milk

3 tbs. Flour

   Cayenne to taste

1 cup grated Swiss Cheese

1 tb. Worcestershire

½ tsp. dry Mustard

1 tsp. Salt

Combine all ingredients except the Shrimp in a saucepan. Stir over medium heat until smooth and creamy. Pour into fondue pot. Into this mixture dip the peeled and cleaned Shrimp.

OLD-FASHIONED FONDUE
(a crabmeat fondue)

½ lb. Butter
4 chopped Onions
1 lb. diced Cheddar Cheese
4 cups Crabmeat

¾ cup Catsup
4 tbs. Worcestershire
¼ cup Sherry
Salt, Pepper to taste

Melt the Butter and sauté the Onions for a few minutes. Add the Cheese, Catsup, Worcestershire, Sherry and Seasonings. Stir constantly until the mixture is smooth. Add the prepared Crabmeat and blend. Serve immediately or refrigerate until ready to serve.

FONDUE JEUNE FILLE

2 ozs. Butter
2 tbs. Flour
1½ cups dry White Wine,
    heated

3 Egg Yolks, some Cream
1 cup freshly grated Swiss Cheese
Nutmeg, Salt, Cayenne to taste

Melt the Butter and add the Flour. Blend well. Slowly add the heated Wine, stirring constantly. When the mixture is thickened, add the Cheese. Stir until the mixture is smooth. Combine the Egg Yolks and Cream and add this to the mixture. Blend well. Stir in the Seasonings and blend.

BERNIE'S FONDUE

½ cup puréed Chicken Livers

½ cup Flour

½ cup Cream

½ cup Tomato Paste

2 tbs. Worcestershire

½ cup Butter

½ cup Parmesan

1 Onion, chopped

1 tsp. Cayenne

¼ cup Cognac

Sauté Onion. Add Flour and stir 5 minutes. Add Cream, Tomato Paste, Salt, Cayenne, Worcestershire, Chicken Livers. Stir until smooth. Cook, stirring constantly for 20 minutes. Remove from heat and add Cheese. Stir until melted. Blend in Cognac.

SIMPLE SIMON

1 lb. diced or coarsely grated Cheddar or American Cheese
½ cup Milk   1 White of Egg
1 tsp. Dry Mustard   1 Egg Yolk

Garlic, Salt, Cayenne or Black Pepper, Paprika to taste. Rub the
bottom and sides of a double-boiler chafing dish with a peeled Garlic
Clove. Put the Cheese into the dish and stir over the flame until it
is smooth. Add the Milk, Seasonings, and Yolk of Egg. Stir well.
Carefully fold in the White of Egg.

EGG FONDUE

¾ cup white Wine
1 Garlic Clove
6 Eggs, beaten

8 oz. grated Cheese
2 tbs. Butter
Salt and Pepper to taste

Press the Garlic Clove into the Wine and heat to boiling. Boil until the liquid is reduced to one-half. This may be done on the stove and brought to the fondue ensemble when ready. In a chafing dish, combine the Cheese, beaten Eggs and Seasonings. Stir until smooth. Add the reduced Wine and blend well.

FONDUE CHABLIS

½ lb. Swiss cheese
1½ tsp. flour
 1 clove garlic
½ cup Chablis

¼ tsp. salt
 pinch pepper
 nutmeg

Grate cheese coarsely and toss with flour. Rub chafing dish and wooden spoon with garlic. Pour in the wine. Heat. Add cheese tossed with flour. Stir until melted. Add seasoning. This recipe makes moderate servings for 3 or 4.

PETITE FONDUE

1 lb. diced Cheese, ½ Swiss and ½ Italian
¾ cup dry White Wine
2 tbs. Brandy
1 clove Garlic, Salt and Pepper to taste

Rub the bottom and sides of a chafing dish with a peeled Garlic Clove. Put in it the diced Cheese and cover with the White Wine. Let stand for 5 hours. A few minutes before serving, heat over a low flame, stirring constantly until smooth. Add the Brandy and Seasonings. Blend.

FONDUTA (an Italian fondue)

¾ lb. Fontina Cheese, diced
   Milk to cover Cheese
¼ tsp. White Pepper

2 tbs. Butter
6 Egg Yolks
1 thinly sliced White Truffle

Combine the Cheese and Milk and let stand 7 hours or overnight. Combine the Egg Yolks, 1 tbs. Butter, the Cheese and Milk mixture in a double boiler-chafing dish. Stir constantly until the mixture becomes very thick and smooth. Remove from the heat. Add the Truffle and Seasonings and the remaining Butter. Blend well.

WITH BEER

8 slices Bread, buttered

8 slices American Cheese

1 tsp. Worcestershire sauce

½ tsp. dry Mustard

1 cup Beer

3 Eggs, beaten

Put buttered Bread, topped with Cheese in a baking dish. Make two layers. Beat together Eggs and seasoning. Stir in Beer. Pour over Bread. Bake in a 350° oven for about 40 minutes.

FONDUE ROUGE

1½ cups sharp American Cheese,   1 tsp. Worcestershire sauce
    coarsely grated   ½ cup condensed Tomato Soup
  ½ cup Bleu Cheese   2 tbs. Sherry

Combine Cheeses, Worcestershire, and Soup. Stir constantly over low heat until Cheese is melted and mixture is creamy. Add Wine and blend well. Serves 3 or 4.

WITH CHIVES

½ lb. grated Cheese dredged in flour
   Salt, Pepper and Nutmeg to taste
  1 cup dry white Wine

3½ tbs. chopped Chives
3 tbs. Butter
2 Egg Yolks

Sauté the Chives in Butter for a few minutes. Add the Wine and heat until bubbly (but not boiling!). Add the Cheese and stir until smooth. Add 3 tbs. of the Cheese mixture to the well beaten Egg Yolks; then pour the Yolk mixture back into the Cheese. Season to taste and blend well.

A FONDUE GARNISH

2 or 3 medium-sized Tomatoes   1 tbs. minced Scallion
   Salt, Cayenne to taste   1½ tbs. Butter

Boil the Tomatoes for 15 seconds. Remove the skins and halve them. Squeeze out the juice and seeds, and cut the pulp into small pieces. Melt the Butter in a saucepan and add the Scallions. Sauté for a few minutes. Stir in the Tomatoes. Cook for 5 or 10 minutes and then add the Seasonings. Blend well. This Garnish may be served with your favorite fondue.

⅔ cups shredded Bleu Cheese

39

CIDER FONDUE

2 lbs. grated cheddar cheese

2 cups dry cider

1 tsp. corn flour

1 tsp. dry mustard

salt, pepper to taste

Blend the corn flour and mustard with ½ cup cider. Melt butter in a saucepan. Add the cheese and remaining cider. Stir constantly over low heat until mixture is melted and smooth. Add corn flour mixture and seasonings. Blend well. Pour into fondue pot and serve.

WITH CHEDDAR CHEESE

1 tb. dry mustard

2 tbs. water

3 tbs. butter

3 tbs. flour

pepper to taste

1 cup milk

2 cups diced cheddar cheese

Mix mustard and water. Let stand for 15 minutes while preparing other ingredients. Melt butter in double boiler. Add flour and pepper. Mix. Slowly stir in milk until thick. Add diced cheese. Stir well until melted. Add mustard mixture and blend. Serves four.

FONDUE PATTIES

1 cup grated Cheese, ½ Swiss, ½ Italian   3 Egg Yolks

2 cups very heavy White Sauce   ½ cup Bread Crumbs

1 Egg beaten with 1 tsp. Oil   Salt, Pepper to taste

Put the Cheese and heavy White Sauce in a saucepan. Stir constantly until the Cheese is melted. Remove from the heat. Add the slightly beaten Egg Yolks and stir well. Cool the mixture. Shape into patties. Roll in the beaten Egg and Oil mixture and dip in the Bread Crumbs. Fry in deep fat until golden brown.

VARIATIONS OF
THE CLASSIC FONDUE

GORGONZOLA ET TILSITER

Identical to The Classic Fondue but use ⅓ Gruyere, ⅓ Gorgonzola, and ⅓ Tilsiter for the cheese.

THE VERMOUTH

Identical to The Classic Fondue but instead of Kirsch use Vermouth.

FONDUE AU BEURRE

Identical to The Classic Fondue but use Butter and Gruyere cheese only. Sauté Garlic. Add Wine. Prepare according to Classic recipe.

45

BAKED FONDUES

LEEK FONDUE

6 slices bread
3 eggs, beaten well
  soft butter
3 cups milk
1½ cups shredded sharp cheddar cheese

¾ tsp. dry mustard
¾ tsp. salt
2 tbs. diced leeks
pepper to taste

Butter bread and cut into pieces. Place in a baking dish. Spread cheese evenly over bread. Combine remaining ingredients and pour over bread. Let stand 2 hours. Bake in 350° oven for 40 minutes. Serves 6.

BAKED BEER FONDUE

1 cup Milk

2 tsp. Caraway Seeds

2½ cups Bread Cubes

4 Eggs, separated

1 cup Beer, 2 tbs. chopped Onion

2 tbs. Butter, ½ tsp. Dry Mustard

1 tsp. Salt, 3 cups grated Cheddar or American Cheese

Scald the combined Milk and Onion. Add the Beer, Salt, Mustard, Cheese and 2 cups of Bread Cubes. Stir until the Cheese has melted. Stir in the beaten Egg Yolks. Fold in the stiffly beaten Egg Whites. Pour into a greased casserole. Dot with Butter. Sprinkle with Seeds and remaining Cubes. Bake 1¼ hours at 325°F.

WITH RICE

2 cups grated sharp Cheese   1 tsp. Salt

1½ cups Milk   Cayenne or Black Pepper to taste

2 cups cooked Rice   4 Eggs, separated

Beat the Egg Yolks well. Mix together the grated Cheese, Milk, Cooked Rice and Seasonings. Add to the Egg Yolks and blend well. Fold in the Egg Whites which have been beaten stiff but not dry. Pour into a greased casserole dish. Bake in a pan of hot water in a 350°F. oven for 1 hour or until done.

A FONDUE MOLD

3 cups shredded Cheddar Cheese

⅔ cups shredded Blue Cheese

½ cup softened Butter

1 tsp. Worcestershire

2 tbs. diced Onion

2 tbs. Chili Sauce

¼ cup dry White Wine

4 tbs. Kirsch

Melt the Butter and blend in the Cheeses. Add the Onion, Wine, Worcestershire and Chili Sauce. Stir constantly over a low flame until the mixture is smooth. Remove from the flame and add the Kirsch. Cool for 20 minutes. Pour into a fluted mold and chill until firm.

GREEN FONDUE (a spinach fondue)

4 Eggs, separated	4 tbs. Butter, ½ tsp. Salt
⅔ cup American Cheese	1⅓ cups Milk
1 cup cooked chopped Spinach	1⅓ cups Bread Crumbs

Heat the Milk and soak the Bread Crumbs in it. Add the Salt and melted Butter. Add the Egg Yolks which have been beaten until creamy. Cook in a double boiler until thick. Cool. Add the chopped Spinach and Cheese. Stir well. Fold in the Egg Whites which have been beaten stiff. Pour into a buttered casserole and bake in a pan of hot water at 350°F. for 1 hour.

FONDUE SANS VIN

6 Eggs, Bread slices for 8
1¾ lbs. sharp grated Cheese
2½ cups Half 'n Half
1 tsp. Brown Sugar, ½ tsp.
Beau Monde

1 tbs. minced Onion, ½ tsp.
Worcestershire
½ tsp. Dry Mustard, Salt, Pepper
to taste

Butter and dice the Bread and arrange on the bottom of a buttered casserole dish. Add a layer of Cheese, one of Bread and the remaining Cheese. Beat the Eggs and add all the other ingredients. Blend well and pour this mixture over the Cheese to just cover. Chill. Before serving, let stand for 1 hour. Bake at 300°F. for about 1 hour.

FONDUE SEC

1 cup Bread Crumbs

½ lb. grated Cheese

1 tbs. Butter, 2 cups Milk

2 Eggs, Salt, Pepper to taste

Preheat the oven to 350°F. Combine the Bread Crumbs and Milk. Stir well. Combine the beaten Eggs, melted Butter, grated Cheese and Seasonings. Add this to the Bread Crumbs and blend together well. Pour into a buttered casserole dish or in individual ramekins and sprinkle the top (or tops) with Bread Crumbs. Bake at 300°F. for 1 hour or until golden brown.

FROZEN
ASPARAGUS

MUSTARD

ASPARAGUS GLACE

1 pkg. (10 oz.) frozen asparagus,
   thawed
3 slices bread, cubed
½ cup grated cheese
1 beaten egg
1 cup milk

½ tsp. salt
½ tsp. pepper
1 tsp. minced onion
1 tbs. butter, melted

Allow asparagus to stand in refrigerator until thawed. Arrange layers of bread, asparagus, and cheese in greased casserole, ending with layer of cheese. Mix together egg, milk, salt, pepper, and onion. Pour over layers. Again, top with cheese. Bake 45 minutes at 350°. Serves four.

WITH CORN

1 cup canned Corn

1 cup grated American Cheese

1½ cups Bread Crumbs

1 cup Milk, 1 tbs. Butter

3 Eggs, separated

Salt, Pepper, Paprika to taste

Combine the Milk, Corn, Cheese, Butter, Bread Crumbs and Seasonings. Stir well. Add the Egg Yolks which have been beaten until creamy. Fold in the Egg Whites which have been beaten stiff but not dry. Bake in a buttered casserole dish or in individual buttered ramekins in a 350°F. oven for 1 hour or until done.

FONDUE POULE (a chicken fondue)

1 undiluted can condensed Cream of Chicken Soup
1 cup grated Cheddar Cheese   4 Eggs, separated
2 cups Bread Crumbs   Salt, Cayenne, Paprika to taste

Preheat the oven to 325°F. Beat the Egg Yolks until lemon yellow.
Add the Bread Crumbs, Cheese, Seasonings and Chicken Soup.
Mix well. Fold in the Egg Whites which have been beaten stiff but
not dry. Pour into a buttered casserole dish. Bake at 325°F. for 1
hour or until done.

THANKSGIVING FONDUE

2 cups diced Turkey

1 cup Turkey Stock

1¾ cups Bread Crumbs

5 Eggs, separated

1 cup Milk, 2 tbs. Butter

¼ tsp. Salt, ¼ tsp. fresh ground
Pepper, 2 tbs. Lemon Juice

1 tsp. fresh ground Thyme

Heat the Milk, Stock and Butter. Add the Turkey, Bread Crumbs, Spices and Juice. Blend well. Stir in the beaten Egg Yolks until thickened. Remove from heat. Fold in the stiffly beaten Egg Whites. Bake in a casserole in a pan of hot water 1¼ hours at 325°F.

NEW ORLEANS FONDUE (a salmon fondue)

1 8 oz. can Salmon

6 slices American Cheese

¼ cup Mayonnaise

12 slices Bread, without crusts

1 tbs. Dry Mustard, ¼ tsp. Salt

3 Eggs, beaten, 2½ cups Milk

1 cup minced Celery, 2 tsp.

Worcestershire

Drain and flake the Salmon and remove the bones. Add the Celery and Mayonnaise blended with the Mustard and Salt. Line a casserole with 6 sandwiches made with this. Top with Cheese. Pour over the combined Eggs, Milk and Worcestershire. Bake 45 minutes at 325°F.

WITH PARMESAN

2 tbs. Butter
1 tb. Flour
½ cup Milk
3 Eggs

¼ lb. grated Parmesan
Salt, Pepper, Cayenne
to taste

Melt Butter and mix in Flour. Add Milk. Mix and cook well. Add seasoning. Beat in 2 Egg yolks. Then stir in grated Cheese until melted. Stir in 3 Egg whites beaten stiff. Put mixture in a baking dish, buttered. Bake for 25 minutes or until firm in middle.

LEARNED FONDUE

1 cup Bread Crumbs

1 Egg, separated

1 cup grated Cheese

2 tbs. Butter

1 cup Milk

Salt, Cayenne to taste

Soak the Bread Crumbs in the Milk which has been heated. Add the Cheese and Seasonings. Mix well. Slowly stir in the Egg Yolk which has been beaten until creamy. Blend. Fold in the Egg White which has been beaten until stiff but not dry. Pour into a casserole dish. Sprinkle the top with Cheese and bake at 325°F. for 1 hour.

LA FONDUE HESTERE (a tuna fondue)

¾ cup sliced Cheddar Cheese
  1 cup diced fresh celery
  2 tsp. Worcestershire

1 17 oz. can Tuna, 1 tbs. Dry
  Mustard
¼ cup Mayonnaise, 3 beaten
  Eggs, 2½ cups Milk, 12
  slices Bread, ½ tsp. Salt

Mix the Tuna and Celery. Combine the Mayonnaise, Mustard, and Salt and add to the Tuna Mixture. Make sandwiches with the Bread and arrange in a casserole with a slice of Cheese on each. Combine the Eggs, Milk and Worcestershire and pour this over the sandwiches. Bake in a pan of hot water 1 hour at 325°F.

JOANNA'S FONDUE (a crabmeat fondue)

2 cups Milk

5 Eggs, separated

1¾ cups Bread Crumbs

1 cup cubed Cheddar Cheese

¼ cup Butter

½ tsp. Salt, ½ tsp. Pepper

¼ tsp. minced Garlic, ½ tsp. minced Onion, ¼ tsp. ground Ginger

17 oz. can flaked Crabmeat

Heat the milk and combine with the Butter, Bread Crumbs, Crabmeat and Spices. Add the beaten Egg Yolks and stir until thickened. Stir in the Cheese until smooth. Fold in the stiffly beaten Egg Whites. Pour into a buttered casserole and bake 1½ hours at 325°F.

FONDUE MARIA

1 cup scalded Milk
1 cup Bread Crumbs
¼ lb. diced Cheese

3 Eggs, separated, 1 tbs. Butter
Salt, Cayenne and Paprika to
taste

Rub the bottom and sides of a casserole with a peeled Garlic Clove. Combine the hot Milk, Bread Crumbs, Butter, Cheese and Seasonings in a double boiler. Stir until smooth. Remove from heat and stir in the beaten Egg Yolks. Blend. Fold in the stiffly beaten Egg Whites. Pour into the casserole. Bake 30-45 minutes at 350°F.

PARISIAN FONDUE

1½ loaves French Bread   ½ cup Butter, 4 beaten Eggs
  ½ cup prepared Mustard   1½ tsp. Worcestershire
1½ lbs. sliced Cheddar Cheese   Salt, Cayenne and Paprika
  5 cups hot Milk   to taste

Spread the Bread with Butter and Mustard. Arrange in a casserole and alternate layers of Cheese and then more Bread. Pour over this the combined Eggs, Milk, Worcestershire and Seasonings. Chill overnite. Bake 1½ hours at 350°F.

FONDUES WITH MEAT

As was mentioned earlier, Beef Fondue is a misnomer. None-theless, meat dishes that involve table cooking from a single pot by individual guests have acquired the fondue label. One such dish is Beef Bourguignonne. This interesting and elegant meal is simple to make, highly visual, and delicious.

The basic elements are lean beef cubes about 1 inch square and peanut oil. Some recipes call for filet but top round can be used if it is tenderized previously. The oil is heated until bubbly. The meat is then submerged on a fondue fork until done to taste. In order for the meat to cook quickly and evenly the oil should remain quite hot.

For this reason a cast iron pot or similar vessel that retains heat well should be used. (Pottery chafing dishes are definitely not satisfactory.) Remember, when spearing the meat the fork should penetrate through the meat about one quarter inch. This allows only the fork to touch the bottom of the pot and prevents sticking. After cooking, the meat is dipped into a sauce and eaten. Special Beef Bourguignonne plates may be purchased that have sections for the various sauces. However, these are not an absolute must.

The sauces that accompany meat fondues allow you to add your own ideas and thus personalize the meal. Choose among the following recipes or make up your own.

FONDUE BOURGUIGNONNE (with sausage)

½ lb. smoked sausage, fully cooked   oil
½ lb. Swiss cheese   2 tbs. butter

Cut the sausage and the cheese into equal size cubes. Put 1½ inches of oil in the fondue pot. Add the butter and bring this oil mixture to a boil. Spear the cheese and the sausage. Dip into the hot fat just long enough to warm both sausage and cheese.

CAPER SAUCE

1 cup Mayonnaise

¼ cup drained Sour Pickle Relish

1 tb. drained chopped Capers

1½ tsp. prepared Mustard

1½ tsp. chopped Parsley

Mix all ingredients. Chill about 1 hour before serving.

ANCHOVY DIP

Mix:

1 cup Mayonnaise

1 tb. chopped Parsley

1 tb. Capers

1 tb. chopped Anchovies

1 hard-cooked Egg, finely
chopped

1 tsp. dry Mustard
Garlic Powder

MUSHROOM

 3 tbs. Butter
½ lb. fresh Mushrooms, chopped
 1 tb. Flour

1 tsp. Soy Sauce
¾ cup Cream

Sauté Mushrooms briefly in Butter. Add Flour and toss. Cook for about 8-10 minutes. Add Soy Sauce. Stir in Cream. Cook, stirring constantly, until mixture thickens. Season to taste.

CURRY MAYONNAISE

½ cup Mayonnaise
½ cup sour Cream

Lemon Juice
Curry Powder

Mix together Mayonnaise and sour Cream. Add Lemon juice and Curry powder to taste.

SOUR CREAM MUSTARD

Mix together:

½ pt. sour Cream

  3 tbs. prepared Mustard

2 tbs. chopped green Onions

Salt

Pepper

ROQUEFORT

¼ lb. Roquefort

½ cup Butter

  1 tb. prepared Mustard

1 clove Garlic, crushed

3 drops Bitters

Blend ingredients. Cover and chill. Let stand an hour or so to soften before serving.

SOUR CREAM HORSERADISH

Mix and chill:

1 cup sour Cream

3 tbs. prepared Horseradish
  well-drained

¼ tsp. Salt

    dash Paprika

CHINESE SWEET AND SOUR

Heat:
½ cup Pineapple Juice   *1 tsp. Soy Sauce*
3 tbs. Oil   *½ tsp. Pepper*
2 tbs. brown Sugar   *¼ cup mild Vinegar*

Thicken with a little cornstarch before serving.

Other popular sauces that go well with Beef Bourguignonne are Béarnaise, Bordelaise, and Cumberland.

Suitable relishes are chutney, bottled horseradish, pickle relish, hot or mild mustard, chopped onion.

From among the sauces and relishes suggested or from your own recipe file, choose at least four in order to provide good variety. Bon appetit!

FONDUE NOEL (a sausage fondue)

2 tbs. minced green Onion

1½ lbs. Pork Sausage

¼ cup Chopped Pimiento

2 tsp. Worcestershire

6 Eggs, beaten, 3 cups Milk

1 tsp. Dry Mustard

12 slices Bread, without crusts

Salt and Pepper to taste

Sauté the Sausage. Add the Onion, Pimiento, Salt, Pepper and Mustard. Blend. Line a casserole with 6 slices of Bread. Cover with the Sausage and a second slice of Bread. Combine the Eggs, Milk, Salt and Worcestershire. Pour this over. Bake 1½ hours at 325°F.

DESSERT FONDUE

A dessert fondue will top off any meal with a special feeling of fellowship. Into these tastey blends of chocolate and other confections dip chunks of angel food cake, lady fingers, pound cake, or bite-size cream-puff pastry. Fresh fruit is also delicious: strawberries, grapes, banana, papaya. Canned fruit may also be used. Be sure to drain well. A little bit of care and imagination in arranging will make any of these dessert fondues a colorful and unusual way to finish a meal.

FONDUE AU CHOCOLAT

Chocolate fondue is actually an American invention. It is said to have been originated in a New York restaurant. There are many variations of the fundamental recipe. The basic ingredients and instructions are as follows:

9 oz. Swiss chocolate, broken into pieces
½ cup whipping cream
Combine ingredients in a chafing dish. Stir over low heat until mixture is melted and smooth.

VARIATIONS

—For variety add ½ cup crushed almonds.

—If you like, add 2 tablespoons kirsh.

—Or add 1 tablespoon instant coffee.

—For a spicier fondue add ¼ teaspoond ground cinnamon and ¼ teaspoon ground cloves.

—Children love to dip marshmallows in the basic combination of chocolate and cream.

—Or use bittersweet chocolate instead of milk chocolate.

—The varieties of Fondue au Chocolat are infinite, limited only by your own personal taste.

FONDUE AU CREME, for dessert or brunch

Mix equal parts of powdered sugar and whipping cream in a sauce-pan. (About 1 cup each for four people.) Bring to boil, stirring constantly. Let boil for about half a minute. Pour into fondue pot or chafing dish and serve. Keep over very low heat to prevent scorching. For variety add flavor by including almond extract, lemon extract, or whatever suits your taste. Food coloring may also be added for special, festive occasions.

CHEDDAR CHEESE WITH GREEN APPLES

3 tsb. butter

3 tbs. flour

1 cup milk

2 cups diced sharp Cheddar cheese

Melt butter in fondue pot. Slowly add the flour. Mix. Slowly stir in the milk until mixture become thick. Add diced cheese, a little at a time. Stir until melted. Into this cheese mixture dip bite-size chunks of crisp, green apples.

RAREBITS

A rarebit, or rabbit, as it is prepared today, is very similar to fondue. Originally, the bread was toasted, then soaked in wine, then covered with cheese, and then toasted again. The result was similar to a grilled sandwich. Today the cheese is melted, as with fondue, and then poured over the toasted bread. There is no reason why, if you so desire, you couldn't dip the bread in the rarebit instead.

The controvery over the name will probably last for as long as people enjoy eating the dish. Some say that it is called rarebit because it is a "rare bit" of gastronomic delight. Others insist that it be called rabbit since it was supposedly originated as a substitute for rabbit. But the stories that support this theory vary. According to some, when a Welsh nobleman ran out of game for his table he served his guests the cheese dish and christened it Welsh Rabbit. Others say that Welsh wives made up the dish and the name to chide husbands who came home from the hunt without any rabbit. Since the controversy is apparently unsolvable, call it what you will. But whatever you call it, surely you will agree that it is a rare bit of eating pleasure.

LONDON RAREBIT

3 tbs. sifted Flour

1½ cup diced Cheddar Cheese

3 tbs. Butter

¼ cup Sherry

½ cup Milk, 1 cup Ale

½ tsp. Salt

Dash Tobasco Sauce

English Toast

Melt the Butter in a double boiler. Add the Flour and Seasonings. Slowly add the Milk and stir until thickened. Remove from heat, and add the Sherry. Blend well. Stir in the Cheese until smooth. Add the Ale and blend.

SPICED RAREBIT

1 lb. diced American Cheese
½ cup Ale, 1 tsp. Mustard
1 tbs. chopped Green Peppers

1 tbs. chopped Spanish Pimientos
Salt, Cayenne and Paprika to
taste

Heat the Cheese until it has melted, stirring until smooth. Add the Mustard and Seasonings. Slowly stir in the Ale. Blend and add the Peppers and Pimientos.

MODERN WELSH RAREBIT

2 lbs. diced American or Cheddar Cheese

1 cup Ale

1 tbs. Butter

½ tsp. Dry Mustard

½ tsp. Salt

1 tsp. Worcestershire

1 tbs. minced Onion

Paprika and Pepper to taste

A very quick rarebit! Melt the Butter and Cheese in a double boiler, stirring constantly. Add the Onion, Worcestershire, Ale, Mustard and Seasonings. Stir the mixture until smooth and of the desired thicknesses.

SHERRY RAREBIT

⅓ cup Cream

1 lb. cubed American Cheese

⅓ cup Sherry

½ tsp. Worcestershire

1 tsp. Dry Mustard

Heat the Cheese in a double boiler until some of the Cheese has melted. Add the Cream and stir until the mixture is smooth. Add the Sherry, stirring until the mixture is smooth. Then add the Worcestershire and Dry Mustard. Stir, and blend well.

92

WESTERN RAREBIT

1½ cups Milk   2 tbs. Butter, 2 tbs. Flour
¼ lb. Dried Beef   2 Eggs, ¼ tsp. Pepper
1 4 oz. package of Pimiento American Cheese, diced

Shred the Beef and rinse it with boiling water. Melt the Butter in a double boiler. Add the Flour and blend. Add the Milk slowly, stirring until thick. Add the Cheese and Beef. Mix until the Cheese melts. Add a little of the mixture to a beaten Egg and pour this into the double boiler. Season to taste and blend well.

OYSTER RAREBIT

1 lb. Cheddar Cheese   ½ tsp. Salt
1 cup Oysters   1 tsp. Worcestershire
1 cup Ale   1 tbs. minced Onion
1 tbs. Butter   1 chopped Green Pepper
½ tsp. Dry Mustard   Paprika and Pepper to taste

Melt the Butter and Cheese in a double boiler, stirring well. Add the Onion, Pepper, Worcestershire, Ale, Mustard and Seasonings, and finally the Oysters. Stir until the mixture is smooth and thick.

RAREBIT A LA CREME

½ lb. diced American or Cheddar Cheese

½ cup Heavy Cream   ¼ tsp. Salt

1 beaten Egg   Pinch of Dry Mustard

2 tbs. Butter   Dash of Chili Powder

Melt the Butter in a saucepan or chafing dish. Add the Cheese and stir until it has melted. Combine the Egg, Cream and Seasonings. Add a little of the Cheese mixture to it and blend. Then pour the Eggs into the Cheese. Stir until smooth and of the desired thickness.

TUNA RAREBIT

1 lb. diced Cheddar Cheese

1 cup canned Tuna

1 cup Ale

1 tbs. Butter

½ tsp. Dry Mustard

½ tsp. Salt

1 tsp. Worcestershire

1 tbs. minced Onion

Paprika and Pepper to taste

Melt the Butter and Cheese in a double boiler, stirring constantly until the Cheese has melted. Add the Onion, Worcestershire, Ale, Mustard and Seasonings and finally Tuna. Stir until the mixture is smooth and thick.

QUICK RAREBIT

1 lb. diced Cheddar Cheese

1 tbs. Chili Sauce

1 tbs. Butter

6 or 7 tbs. Ale

1 tsp. Tabasco Sauce

Mustard, Salt and Pepper to taste

Melt the Butter in a saucepan or chafing dish. Slowly add the Diced Cheese and stir until the Cheese has melted. Add the Tabasco Sauce, Mustard and Seasonings and blend well. Add the Ale little by little, stirring constantly. Blend and stir until the mixture is smooth and of the desired thickness.

CREAM OF CELERY RAREBIT

1 10 oz. undiluted can of Cream of Celery Soup
1½ cups diced Cheddar Cheese   ½ tsp. Mustard, 1 Egg, separated
¼ cup dry White Wine   ½ tsp. Worcestershire

Combine the Soup, Mustard, Wine and Worcestershire in a saucepan or chafing dish. Heat until just beginning to boil. Slowly add the Cheese, stirring constantly until the Cheese has melted and the mixture is blended. Mix in the well beaten Egg and stir until the mixture is of the thickness desired.

FRANK RAREBIT

1 Onion, sliced
2 cups shredded American Cheese
2 tbs. Butter

5 Frankfurters
¾ cup Milk
5 slices buttered Toast

Melt the Butter in a saucepan and sauté the Frankfurters for 15 minutes. Meanwhile combine the Cheese and Milk in a double boiler, stirring constantly until the Cheese has melted and the mixture is smooth and of the desired thickness. Slit the Frankfurters up the middle, and place them on buttered Toast. Pour the Cheese over them and garnish with Onions.

CALIFORNIA SHRIMP RAREBIT

1 10 oz. can of Cream of Shrimp Soup
¼ cup California Sherry
1 lb. diced Cheddar Cheese
Salt and Pepper to taste

Melt the Cheese slightly in a double boiler. Add the Soup and stir until the Cheese has completely melted and the mixture is smooth. Slowly, blend in the Sherry and mix until the mixture is of the desired thickness. Add the Seasonings and blend well.

SPANISH RAREBIT

3 tbs. Butter

½ cup chopped Onions

1 Garlic Clove

2 chopped Green Peppers

1 cup Beer

¼ tsp. Tabasco Sauce

2 cups grated American Cheese

Melt the Butter in a saucepan or chafing dish. Chop the Peppers and Onions well and sauté them with the crushed Garlic Clove for 5 minutes. Slowly add the grated Cheese, stirring constantly until smooth. Add the Beer and Tabasco Sauce and blend well.

EASTERN RAREBIT

1 can Sardines
1 tbs. Butter
   Salt, Pepper to taste
   a Cheese Rarebit

Remove the bones from the Sardines. Melt the Butter in a saucepan and sauté them for about 10 minutes. Season to taste and spoon the Butter over them. Then place them on English toast and pour your favorite Cheese Rarebit over them.

102

ROSY RAREBIT

1 6 oz. can Tomatoes
1½ tbs. Butter
1 lb. American Cheese, diced
Salt and Pepper to taste

Drain the Tomatoes. Melt the Butter in a saucepan and add the Tomatoes and Seasonings. Sauté about 25 minutes and then slowly add the Cheese, stirring constantly until it has melted. When the mixture is of the thickness desired, readjust the Seasonings and blend well.

BEAN RAREBIT

1 cup mashed baked Beans with Tomato Sauce

2 tbs. Butter   1 tsp. Salt

⅔ cup grated Cheddar Cheese   1 cup Milk

¼ tsp. Paprika   1 tsp. A-1 or Worcestershire

Melt the Butter and slowly add the Cheese, stirring constantly until the Cheese is melted. Add the Beans and the Seasonings. Stir until the mixture is creamy. Slowly add the Milk, and stir until the Rarebit is of the desired thickness.